2022

Savannah

The Restaurant Enthusiast's Discriminating Guide

Andrew Delaplaine

Andrew Delaplaine is the Food Enthusiast.
When he's not playing tennis,
he dines anonymously
at the Publisher's (considerable) expense.

James Cubby – Senior Editor

The Restaurant Enthusiast's
Discriminating Guide

Table of Contents

INTRODUCTION

Every time I visit Savannah, I ask myself the same question: what is it about this fair city that I like so much?

An impossible question (for me) to answer. The culture? The food (Ah, yes, the food!)? The people? The charming layout of the city?

It's all of those things, of course. Savannah is a much more interesting city than Charleston because you can basically see what there is to see in Charleston in a day. A Long Weekend is more than ample time to savor the riches of Charleston (excluding its numerous fine restaurants) unless you venture to some of the plantations outside town.

Not so Savannah. You'll need a lot more than a Long Weekend to take in everything Savannah has to offer, trust me.

Of all historic figures, Civil War General William Sherman is largely responsible for preserving the city by the simple act of *not* burning it down when he made his famous March to the Sea, destroying everything in his Army's path—except Savannah.

My first experience here was as an undergrad when I came to meet the parents of my college girlfriend. Theirs was one of the older families in Savannah, and their name even graces one of its most famous squares.

Speaking of those famous squares, the layout of Savannah makes it very interesting. There are 21 squares that give this city a strong human scale other U.S. cities will never have. Savannah feels more like London than any other American city to my mind (except of course for the weather). These squares, sometimes frustrating for motorists who have to navigate around them, make cycling around Savannah a pleasure.

There used to be 24 squares in the original plan of the city, but 3 of these were sacrificed to developers who demolished them before the people came to their senses and stopped the wanton destruction of Savannah's valuable heritage. Another square, Ellis, once no more than a parking lot, is now looking more like it did in the old days.

A little side note: famed lyricist Johnny Mercer, who wrote some 1,600 songs and took home 4 Oscars for Best Song, was from here. He was one of the great contributors to the Great American Songbook. (He wrote “Moon River,” for example, which Audrey Hepburn sang not so well in “Breakfast at Tiffany’s.”)

Be certain to visit the **River Street Pedestrian District**. Here you’ll see water taxis, riverboats, and numerous private craft plying the river. The waterfront is lined with shops, restaurants and quite a few tourist traps. Still, it’s great to see it.

GETTING ABOUT

CAR

Unless you're going to be staying downtown in the Historic District, you will need a car.

PUBLIC TRANSIT

CAT
Chatham Area Transit
www.catchacat.org
Bus service throughout Savannah. There's a free **CAT Shuttle** (Route #1) that serves the Historic District.

STREETCAR
CONNECTONTHEDOT

www.connectonthedot.com

The River Street Streetcar runs 1 mile along an old streetcar line in the Downtown Historic District. It has 12 stops on its route.

FERRY

There's a free **Savannah Belles Ferry** that runs across the Savannah River, linking the Historic District and Convention Center on Hutchinson Island.

WALKING

In the Historic District, you can do a lot of walking. Park your car and go out on foot.

Information:

www.savannahvisit.com

MLK Visitor Information Center

301 Martin Luther King, Jr. Blvd., Savannah, 912-944-0455

www.visitsavannah.com/profile/mlk-visitor-information-center/6155

Tybee Island Visitor Information Center

1st St, Tybee Island, 912-786-5444

www.visittybee.com/travel-aid/tybee-visitor-center

Visitor Center at Ellis Square
26 Barnard St, Savannah, 912-525-3100 x 1343

Savannah/ Hilton Head International Airport Visitor Center
400 Airways Ave, Savannah, 912-964-0514
www.savannahairport.com/at-the-airport/visitor-information-center

Visit Savannah Visitor Information Center
101 E Bay St, Savannah, 912-644-6400
www.visitsavannah.com

The River Street Visitor Information Center
1 W River St, Savannah, 912-651-6662
www.visit-historic-savannah.com/savannah-visitor-center.html

The A to Z Listings

Ridiculously Extravagant
Sensible Alternatives
Quality Bargain Spots

45 BISTRO
123 E Broughton St, Savannah, 912-234-3111
www.45bistro.com

CUISINE: American
DRINKS: Full Bar
SERVING: Dinner
PRICE RANGE: $$$

Located adjacent to the historic Marshall House, here you'll enjoy some of Savannah's finest dining. Chef Ryan Behneman prepares dishes like lasagna of jumbo sea scallops, wilted spinach, mascarpone cheese and a tomato ragu and filet of salmon gratinéed with sautéed hearts of palm and artichokes.

700 DRAYTON
Mansion on Forsyth Park
700 Drayton St., Savannah: 912-721-5002
www.mansiononforsythpark.com

The she-crab bisque here has lumps of crab meat and they aren't shy with the sherry. While they have a fine selection of steaks here, I'd focus on the Southern specialties: crispy chicken livers, pan-fried crab cakes, shrimp fritters, things of this sort, because they do such a good job. I'm nuts about this place.

A-J's DOCKSIDE RESTAURANT
1315 Chatham Ave, Tybee Island, 912-786-9533
www.ajsdocksidetybee.com
CUISINE: Seafood
DRINKS: Full Bar
SERVING: Dinner
PRICE RANGE: $$
Tucked into a quiet waterfront corner on the island's south side. Here you'll find some of the best seafood on the island. Try favorites like the shrimp and grits or artichoke dip appetizers, or a bowl of crab stew or scored flounder. Arrive early for dinner.

BACK IN THE DAY BAKERY
2403 Bull St, Savannah, 912-495-9292
www.backinthedaybakery.com
An old-fashioned bakery that's a favorite among locals, tourists and foodies. Not just a bakery but also a café with a delicious menu of sandwiches, like the Madras curry chicken on ciabatta. Here you'll find Savannah's best desserts, artisan breads, award winning cupcakes along with great coffee and espresso. Free Wifi.

BOAR'S HEAD GRILL & TAVERN
1 N Lincoln St, Savannah, 912-651-9660
www.boarsheadgrillandtavern.com
CUISINE: American
DRINKS: Full Bar
SERVING: Lunch & Dinner
PRICE RANGE: $$

Located in the historic section of Savannah, Chef Philip Branan prepares a delicious selection of steaks, chops and seafood.

CLARY'S CAFÉ
404 Abercorn St, Savannah, 912-233-0402
www.claryscafe.com
Steeped in local history, Clary's, in business since 1903, serves breakfast all day including omelets, grits, steaming biscuits and plain, pecan strawberry and blueberry malted waffles. The restaurant is covered with knickknacks, paintings, family pictures and memorabilia.

COLLINS QUARTER
2 locations
151 Bull St, Savannah, 912-777-4147
621 Drayton St, Savannah, 912-298-6544
https://www.thecollinsquarter.com/
CUISINE: Breakfast/American (New) / Australian
DRINKS: Full Bar
SERVING: Breakfast, Lunch, & Dinner – No Dinner on Mondays & Tuesdays
PRICE RANGE: $$
NEIGHBORHOOD: Historic District
Two coffee cafes serving brunch all day and creative lunch and dinner options. It's more a spirited café during the day, but at night they light candles to give the place a more intimate, romantic aura. Favorites: Aussie Based Avocado Smash; Short Rib Hash is a standout; Ahi Tuna Poke. Innovative cocktails and extensive wine list. Impressive coffee menu. Reservations recommended.

COTTON & RYE
1801 Habersham St, Savannah, 912-777-6286
http://www.cottonandrye.com/
CUISINE: American (New)
DRINKS: Full Bar
SERVING: Dinner (Closed Sundays & Mondays)
PRICE RANGE: $$$
NEIGHBORHOOD: Thomas Square
Set in a former 1950s bank, this gastropub offers a creative menu of New American fare. There's a nice bar inside, but if the weather's nice, I always opt for a table on their outdoor deck. Favorites: Shrimp & Grits and Fried Chicken with Mac and Cheese. (There are many great versions of fried chicken in Savannah, but if this is your first trip, you could do worse than get it here—and since you're getting fried chicken, get their mac & cheese to go with it.) Amazing cocktails.

DECK BEACH BAR AND KITCHEN
404 Butler Ave., Tybee Island, 912-328-5397
www.thedecktybee.com
CUISINE: American (New)/Seafood
DRINKS: Full Bar
SERVING: Lunch & Dinner; Closed Mon – Wed.
PRICE RANGE: $$

Less than a half-hour from Savannah, this is the only bar / restaurant on the sand in Tybee with ocean views from every seat. Favorites: Vietnamese style shrimp Po Boy sandwich and Chicken Satay sandwich. The seafood platter here is big enough to satisfy 2 or even 3. It's tempura cod made with a beer-batter, grilled shrimp, fried calamari, snow crab legs, ahi tuna poke (they say it's ahi tuna, but probably not), corn on the cob, vinegar fries, sweet potato fries and a good portion of island-style cole slaw. (I was with one other person when we ordered it, and we brought home enough to feed another person.) The good thing about this seafood platter is that it's not all fried, like so many others. Vegetarian options. Dining inside or on the deck. Happy hour. The view makes this a great brunch spot. Go for a walk on the beach to work up an appetite. (Note the closed days above.)

ELIZABETH ON 37TH

105 E 37th St, Savannah, 912-236-5547
www.elizabethon37th.net
CUISINE: American
DRINKS: Full Bar
SERVING: Dinner
PRICE RANGE: $$$
Chef Kelly Yambor serves up fresh seafood in an elegant stately mansion dating back to the early 20th

Century. Favorites include the shrimp and grits with red-eye gravy, traditionally made from leftover coffee, Bluffton oysters served three ways, including raw with tomato-cilantro; snapper with a chewy crust of shredded potato and asiago cheese; spicy red rice & shrimp; clams with roasted Vidalia onions. They use house grown herbs and edible flowers in their dishes. There's a 7-course tasting menu available that's a good bet. Excellent service from beginning to end.

EMPORIUM KITCHEN AND WINE MARKET
254 E Perry St., Savannah, 912-559-8400
www.emporiumsavannah.com
CUISINE: American (New)
DRINKS: Full Bar
SERVING: Breakfast, Lunch, & Dinner

PRICE RANGE: $$
Popular eatery offering locally sourced, quality menu items, but it's also part market, part coffee shop, a bistro-style feel to it and a take-away option. Favorites: Local Salmon en Papillote; Roasted BBQ oysters; and Rabbit Ragout with House-Made Pappardelle. Bar on first floor and rooftop, ice cream bar and wine area, and games on rooftop.

FLYING MONK NOODLE BAR
5 W Broughton St, Savannah, 912-232-8888
www.flywiththemonk.com

CUISINE: Vietnamese
DRINKS: Beer & Wine Only
SERVING: Lunch & Dinner
PRICE RANGE: $$

This popular eatery offers a menu restaurant featuring pan-Asian noodle dishes. Noodle dishes from a variety of Asian nations are represented including Vietnam, Malaysia, China, Thailand, Korea, and Laos. Menu favorites include: Pho beef and Peking Duck.

FOX & FIG
321 Habersham St, Savannah, 912-297-6759

https://foxandfigcafe.com/
CUISINE: Vegan/Breakfast
DRINKS: Wine & Beer
SERVING: Breakfast, Lunch, & Dinner
PRICE RANGE: $$
NEIGHBORHOOD: Troup Square
High-end vegan café featuring a variety of vegan options, coffees, milkshakes, and lattes. (Non-dairy.) I'm not big on vegan food as a rule, but my girlfriend loves it, and she really insists on coming here. Favorites: Chipotle Mac & Cheese and the Fox Burger. Outdoor seating. Dog friendly.

FOXY LOXY CAFÉ
1919 Bull St, Savannah, 912-401-0543
www.foxyloxycafe.com
CUISINE: Espresso Bar/Tex-Mex

DRINKS: Beer & Wine
SERVING: Breakfast, Lunch, Desserts
PRICE RANGE: $
A cute little place with a small menu but they serve excellent craft beers and delicious tacos. There's also a nice dessert selection, great coffees and they serve breakfast all day. Live music on Tuesday nights.

It's close & tight at Geneva's, but the food's spectacular.

GENEVA'S FAMOUS CHICKEN AND CORNBREAD CO.
1909 Victory Dr, Savannah, 912-235-2978
https://www.eatgenevas.com/
CUISINE: Southern
DRINKS: No Booze
SERVING: Lunch, & Dinner (Closed Mondays)

PRICE RANGE: $$
NEIGHBORHOOD: Olympus/Victory Square
Small down-home eatery (with only a few tables inside and a couple outside with a handful of chairs at the counter) offering authentic Southern fare focusing on chicken, seafood, and homemade vegetable dishes. This is the real thing, folks. Favorites: Fried Chicken and Mac & Cheese. Most places in the South have "their own" cornbread recipe, which is fine, but here they cleverly offer delicious cornbread in a variety of flavors, such as jalapeño and blueberry, which I really love.

GREEN TRUCK PUB
2430 Habersham St., 912-234-5885
www.greentruckpub.com
CUISINE: Pubs, Burgers
DRINKS: Beer & Wine
SERVING: Lunch, dinner, Tuesday-Saturday
PRICE RANGE: $$

The crew at the Green Truck Pub, just a parking lot away from the Habersham antiques mall, makes simple food from scratch, sourcing as many of their ingredients as they can locally. They use grass-fed beef from Hunter Cattle in nearly Brooklet, and their pork and free-range chicken are raised in Georgia. They buy their coffee beans from Perc Coffee just a few blocks away. Produce is selected at the farmer's market at nearby Forsyth Park. Popular menu items include the Rustico burger with goat cheese, balsamic caramelized onions, roasted red peppers and fresh basil that they grow in their backyard garden; the Whole Farm, a bacon-cheddar burger topped with a fried egg; the California BLT has avocado; one of my favorites here is the Grilled Cheese with bacon and tomato. Add the hand-cut fries and you're all set. They have a rotating selection of about 30 craft beers.

THE GREY
109 Martin Luther King Jr Blvd, Savannah, 912-662-5999
www.thegreyrestaurant.com
CUISINE: American (New) / Bistro
DRINKS: Full Bar
SERVING: Lunch & Dinner; closed Mon
PRICE RANGE: $$$

Located in a sleek refurbished 1938 Greyhound bus depot from the Art Deco era, this high-end eatery offers a pleasing menu of Southern fare from Chef Mashama Bailey. The kitchen was installed in what used to be the ticket booth. Fancy décor with steel-blue booths, terrazzo floors. There was a 24-hour diner in the old bus station that has been remodeled into an elegant bar. The chef was born in the Bronx, but has steeped herself in Southern cuisine. Try her spicy BBQ sauce she slathers on her chicken schnitzel sandwich. Nice wine list with a focus on European labels. This is a good place to begin a night on the town.

GRYPHON TEA ROOM
337 Bull St., Savannah, 912-525-5880
www.scadgryphon.com
CUISINE: Tea Room/American fare
DRINKS: No Booze
SERVING: Lunch & Dinner
PRICE RANGE: $
American café known for their sumptuous tea service that's situated on the wonderful Madison Square in the handsome Scottish Rite Masonic Temple that dates back to 1926. Gryphon is part of the Savannah

College of Art & Design. Though they have a great short menu, including delectable sandwiches, the tea is what you'll want to come here for. Impressive selection of teas served with tea sandwiches, scones and Devonshire cream & jam. That said, I might add they have an excellent brunch menu as well, with a full English breakfast which includes a sweet potato hash that's out of this world. Favorites: Asian-marinated salmon and Maple-glazed pork loin. There's outdoor seating on the red-bricked sidewalk.

HUSK
12 W Oglethorpe Ave., Savannah, 912-349-2600
www.husksavannah.com
CUISINE: Southern/Desserts

DRINKS: Full Bar
SERVING: Lunch & Dinner
PRICE RANGE: $$
Set in a landmark mansion, this elegant eatery offers a menu of Southern fare, but with a unique twist shared by its other outposts in Charleston and Nashville (among other cities). They strive to use the "indigenous ingredients" of coastal Georgia. And they do it so well. As a rule, the first meal I eat when I get to Charleston is at Husk. Now the same is true in Savannah. Menu changes daily, depending on what's available that's fresh and in season. Favorites: Hot Fried Chicken with Bradford Collards; Glazed pork ribs with pickled Georgia peaches (those peaches are SO good); and Mark's Tilefish. Order a side of sour dough bread for the table – you won't be disappointed. Upstairs bar. Nice wine selection.

Interior of HUSK – just one of the rooms

THE LADY AND SONS
102 W Congress St, Savannah, 912-233-2600
www.ladyandsons.com
CUISINE: Southern
DRINKS: Full bar
SERVING: Lunch and dinner daily
PRICE RANGE: $$-$$$
This is the place that launched Paula Deen, the place that inspired her first cookbook that led to stardom on the Food Network. Always a busy place. The sons mentioned are Jamie and Bobby. This 3-floor complex serves some 8,000 or 9,000 people a week. Three separate tour groups offer Paula Deen tours that will take visitors to her restaurant and the one she operates with her brother on Tybee Island as well as some other Deen-related stops. The menu is extensive, one of those "something for everything" kind of menus you see at a national chain. And I don't

particularly like the place because you feel like one of the cattle that end up in the burgers when you come here. This is not to say the food is less than good: crab cakes, crab stuffed Portobello, fried green tomatoes, black pepper shrimp, fried okra, crab stew cup. There's even an all you can eat Southern Buffet. I do, however, stop in often to buy things from their store. (People love things I get here as gifts.)

LOCAL 11 TEN FOOD & WINE
1110 Bull St, Savannah, 912-790-9000
www.local11ten.com
CUISINE: New Southern
DRINKS: Full bar (excellent wine list)
SERVING: Dinner nightly from 6
PRICE RANGE: $$
Though the building is in an unassuming structure that used to be a bank a block from Forsyth Park, inside you'll find an elegant room with sky-high ceilings, blond paneled walls. The people here insist on listing the farms where the vegetables came from, the company that delivered fish caught that day, the cheesemonger who produced their cheeses, the guy who cured their bacon, the company that made their grits. Maybe they push this element too hard, but the results speak for themselves. They *care* about their food. Try the Caesar's salad here: made with local romaine lettuce, pecorino Romano, olives, bacon bits and their own croutons. You've never had a Caesar's salad like this. The charcuterie board features meats

they cured themselves and even their own pickles. Main courses might include frog legs from North Carolina or Beaufort County octopus with shaved onion and marinated feta, or, one night I was there, I had the milk-braised lamb's belly. Boy, was it tender. Menu changes frequently. Bright idea: do the chef's tasting menu and enjoy the tour. (Wine list here is very good, by the way, one of the best in town.)

MADAME BUTTERFLY
110 W Congress St, Savannah, 912-999-8539
https://www.madamebutterflysavannah.com/
CUISINE: Korean Steakhouse
DRINKS: Full bar
SERVING: Dinner, Lunch on Sat. & Sun.
PRICE RANGE: $$
NEIGHBORHOOD: Historic District
A sleek steakhouse with a clean modern design, this eatery features a variety of Korean style choices including duck, Yakatori skewers, Korean BBQ (one

of my favorites) and Wagu fillet. Some outdoor seating as well. Signature cocktails.

MASADA CAFÉ
2301 W Bay St, Savannah, 912-236-9499
No Website
CUISINE: Southern
DRINKS: No Booze
SERVING: Lunch
PRICE RANGE: $
Located in the United House of Prayer for All People, so you know the food is prepared with love. Here

you'll find no frills Southern cooking and it's all about good home cooked soul food. Order from a simple menu that includes crispy fried chicken, delicious mac 'n cheese, and sweet potatoes served with cinnamon and nutmeg. For the entire experience visit the 11 a.m. Sunday service then stay for lunch.

MRS. WILKES' DINING ROOM
107 W Jones St, Savannah, 912-232-5997
www.mrswilkes.com
CUISINE: Southern / Soul Food
DRINKS: No Booze
SERVING: Lunch – weekdays; closed Sat & Sun
PRICE RANGE: $$
This busy Southern diner offers a family experience as lunch guests dine at communal tables. Tables are covered with dishes like Fried chicken, sweet potato soufflé, black-eyed peas, okra gumbo, corn muffins and biscuits. Menu changes daily.

OLDE PINK HOUSE
23 Abercorn St, Savannah, 912-232-4286
www.plantersinnsavannah.com/the-olde-pink-house/
CUISINE: Southern
DRINKS: Full Bar
SERVING: Lunch, Dinner

PRICE RANGE: $$$
If you love Southern cooking then you must eat here, as the food is to die for. Menu favorites include: Fried Green Tomatoes and the Shrimp & Grits. The setting is lovely and each part of the house has a historical theme. Save room for dessert and have the Chocolate Mouse Bomb.

PACCI ITALIAN KITCHEN + BAR @ THE BRICE HOTEL
601 E Bay St, Savannah, 912-233-6002
www.paccisavannah.com
CUISINE: Italian
DRINKS: Full Bar
SERVING: Breakfast, Lunch & Dinner
PRICE RANGE: $$
This rustic restaurant/bar offers Chef Roberto Leoci's menu of locally sourced Italian cuisine. Menu

favorites include: Prosciutto and Melon and Cubano Italiano – a delicious pasta dish.

RANCHO ALEGRE CUBAN
402 Martin Luther King Jr Blvd, Savannah, 912-292-1656
www.ranchoalegrecuban.com
CUISINE: Cuban/Seafood
DRINKS: Full Bar
SERVING: Lunch & Dinner
PRICE RANGE: $$
No frills but pleasant enough Cuban eatery serving traditional plates of Cuban, Caribbean, Spanish and Latin American fare. (So much for focus.) Favorites: Marinated steak and Paella (if you want Paella put in your order right away as it takes 40 minutes—the

Paella here is prepared Valenciana style—quite delicious and bursting with flavors). Creative cocktails. The "Suicide" cocktail is deadly, LOL. Latin Jazz on the weekends. Wines from the Argentine, since Cuba is mostly known for beer, daiquiris, mojitos, 1950s cars with new engines and lots and lots of potholes. Oh, and outdated Communism.

REPEAL 33
125 Martin Luther King Jr Blvd, Savannah, 912-200-9255

https://www.repeal33savannah.com/
CUISINE: American (New)
DRINKS: Full Bar
SERVING: Dinner, Sunday Brunch
PRICE RANGE: $$
NEIGHBORHOOD: Yamacraw Village
Hip speakeasy-style bar offering a menu of New American fare. Has a long bar that extends down the whole room, and a few bare-bones wooden tables and chairs scattered about. Favorites: City Ham wrapped asparagus Tempura and House-Made Charcuterie. Live music. Reservations recommended.

SANDFLY BBQ
8413 Ferguson Ave, Savannah, 912-356-5463
www.sandflybbq.com
CUISINE: Barbeque
DRINKS: Beer & Wine Only
SERVING: Lunch & Dinner; closed Sun
PRICE RANGE: $$

A popular eatery serving Savannah style BBQ. Here you can sample delicious BBQ sandwiches, combination plates and smoked meats – glorious Southern fare. Excellent ribs and baked beans. The menu also includes a variety of specials of Southwestern, Cajun, and Creole cuisine.

Low Country Boil

SAVANNAH SEAFOOD SHACK
116 E Broughton St, Savannah, 912-344-4393
https://savannahseafoodshack.com/
CUISINE: Seafood
DRINKS: Wine & Beer
SERVING: Lunch, & Dinner
PRICE RANGE: $$
NEIGHBORHOOD: Historic District
Popular fast-casual eatery specializing in Southern-style seafood dishes. Favorites: Spicy Garlic Blue

Crabs; Low Country Boils; Po-boys; and Fried Fish Tacos. Corn on the cob and Hush puppies are standout sides.

SENTIENT BEAN
13 E Park Ave, Savannah, 912-232-4447
www.sentientbean.com
CUISINE: Vegetarian
DRINKS: No Booze
SERVING: Breakfast, Lunch & Dinner (7 a.m. to 10 p.m.)
PRICE RANGE: $
This coffee shop is a treat to visit and the menu if filled with organic, homemade food. This is a vegetarian/vegan's delight serving fresh, local organic foods. Menu consists of salads, tortillas, sandwiches and homemade soups. Breakfast served all day.

There's also live music, film, and open mic nights. Check out the website for the rotating schedule.

SIX PENCE PUB
245 Bull St, Savannah, 912-233-3151
www.sixpencepub.com
CUISINE: American Traditional
DRINKS: Full Bar
SERVING: Lunch & Dinner
PRICE RANGE: $$
Those favoring British-style pubs will feel at home here. The pub eats are strictly English fare and the beer selection is quite impressive.

SOHO SOUTH CAFÉ
12 W Liberty St, Savannah, 912-233-1633
www.sohosouthcafe.com
CUISINE: American
DRINKS: Beer & Wine Only
SERVING: Lunch
PRICE RANGE: $$
This funky café, located in a former auto repair garage, is operated by local artists. Menu includes dishes like eggs Savannah, an English muffin topped with a jumbo crab cake, poached egg, asparagus and béarnaise. Their slogan, and it's appropriate, is "Where Food is Art.""

SUNDAE CAFÉ
304 First St., Tybee Island, 912-786-7694
www.sundaecafe.com
CUISINE: Reinvented Southern
DRINKS: Full bar
SERVING: Lunch, Dinner
PRICE RANGE: $$
Fried green tomatoes are in lots of dishes of this family-owned Tybee Island restaurant: you can get them as an appetizer or on top of salad, a BLT or even a burger. Other favorites: seafood cheesecake, shrimp and grits and a variety of other seafood. Paula Deen is said to like the double-cut pork chop. Speaking of Deen, she's added their recipes for Succotash, Apple Chutney and Buttermilk Biscuit Blue Cheese Bread Pudding in her "Cooking with Paula Deen" magazine.

TREYLOR PARK
115 E Bay St, Savannah, 912-495-5557
https://www.treylorpark.com/
CUISINE: American (New)
DRINKS: Full Bar
SERVING: Lunch, & Dinner
PRICE RANGE: $$
NEIGHBORHOOD: Historic District – North
Quick in-and-out kind of place serving Southern 'comfort food' grub with a few twists, not all of them so great. Favorites: Cheese Steak Egg Rolls; Sloppy Joe and Pot Pie. Get the Bourbon Pecan Pie for dessert. Cocktail bar and some outdoor seating.

VIC'S ON THE RIVER
26 East Bay St, Savannah, 912-721-1000
https://www.vicsontheriver.com/
CUISINE: Southern/Seafood
DRINKS: Full Bar
SERVING: Lunch, & Dinner
PRICE RANGE: $$
NEIGHBORHOOD: Downtown
Overlooking the River, this place is set in disused cotton warehouse built in 1859, now repurposed as a fine-dining eatery specializes in classic Southern fare and seafood. They have several rooms with high ceilings overlooking the water. Expansive windows at street level offer a lovely view of the trees outside.

Favorites: She Crab Soup; Braised Beef Short Rib served with sour cream mash; and Wreckfish. Creative cocktails like the Peach Martini. Save room for the wonderful Praline Cheesecake, which is worth the trip by itself. The Wine Bar and Piano Bar add to the ambiance. Reservations recommended.

VINNIE VAN GO-GO'S
317 W Bryan St, Savannah, 912-233-6394
www.vinnievangogo.com
CUISINE: Pizza
DRINKS: Beer & Wine Only
SERVING: Lunch & Dinner
PRICE RANGE: $
This hugely popular indoor-outdoor pizza joint offers hearty crust pizza. Locals can't get enough of it.

WALL'S BARBECUE
515 E York Ln, Savannah, 912-232-9754
No Website
CUISINE: Barbeque, Soul Food
DRINKS: No Booze
SERVING: Lunch & Dinner; has erratic operating hours, but usually open weekends
PRICE RANGE: $
An out-of-the-way eatery is prized by locals. They only have 3 tables or so but the food is just fine. Thick crab cakes, plates of crab, chicken, fish or pork served with sides of rice, coleslaw, collard greens or okra. The deviled crab is good, and the ribs are excellent, too.

WYLD DOCK BAR
2740 Livingston Ave, Savannah, 912-692-1219
http://www.thewylddockbar.com/
CUISINE: Seafood
DRINKS: Full Bar
SERVING: Lunch & Dinner; Closed Mondays
PRICE RANGE: $$
Waterside eatery serving New American fare about 15 or 20 minutes from Savannah where you'll get an expansive view of marshlands. Fresh seafood daily. Menu changes often, usually every month. Try the Fresh catch and Fish tacos served in banana leaves; Quail & Rabbit Sausage; Shrimp roll. Outdoor dining with waterfront views of the desolate marshlands. Locals' hangout.

ZUNZI'S
236 Drayton St, Savannah, 912-443-9555
www.zunzis.com
CUISINE: International/Sandwiches
DRINKS: No Booze
SERVING: Lunch
PRICE RANGE: $
Closed Sunday
This café offers a mixture of international cuisine (Swiss, Italian, South African, and Dutch). Menu favorites include: The Godfather (an amazing sandwich made of smoked sausage, chicken, cheese, lettuce and tomato) and the Portabella Sandwich. Ideal for a casual lunch on a nice day.

NIGHTLIFE

ALLEY CAT LOUNGE
207 W Broughton St, Savannah, 912-631-8160
https://www.alleycatsavannah.com/
Hip dimly-lit basement bar stocking more than 500 spirits with one of the most impressive cocktail menus in Savannah. Entrance through a door in the back alley, down the stairs to the basement. You'll feel like you're in a speakeasy. Classic cocktails.

AMERICAN LEGION SAVANNAH POST NO 135

1108 Bull St, Savannah, 912-233-9277

www.alpost135.com

A historic structure that was built in 1913, now houses the town's neighborhood bar. No frills bar with cheap drinks.

BETTER THAN SEX

410 W Broughton St, Savannah, 912-306-0309

https://www.betterthansexdesserts.com/location/better-than-sex-savannah/

Intimate dessert restaurant with a speakeasy-style atmosphere. Bar menu features unique items like chocolate and caramel covered wines. Perfect for a date night.

CASIMIR'S LOUNGE
MANSION ON FORSYTH PARK

700 Drayton St., Savannah: 912-721-5002
www.mansiononforsythpark.com

Try to squeeze in a drink at Casimir's, the rooftop lounge above the Mansion on Forsyth Park where you can look out over the Historic District. (Live jazz and blues Fri & Sat nights.) Always a real treat whenever I visit Savannah.

CLUB ONE
1 Jefferson St, Savannah, 912-232-0200
www.clubone-online.com
The site of The Lady Chablis Show until her passing in September 2016. The club still offers cabaret with a variety of performers. Cash only.

CRYSTAL BEER PARLOR

301 W Jones St, Savannah, 912-349-1000

www.crystalbeerparlor.com

This is Savannah's second oldest restaurant and a favorite gathering spot for locals. Simple menu but everything is fresh and prepared to order. Friendly servers and great selection of beers.

ELECTRIC MOON SKYTOP LOUNGE & MOON DECK

500 W River St, Savannah, 912-373-9070
https://www.plantriverside.com/venues/electric-moon-skytop-lounge/
Located on the roof of the JW Marriot Hotel, this rooftop lounge offers stunning river views, signature cocktails, and live music. Bar games and dancing.

LOST SQUARE

412 Williamson St, Savannah, 912-715-7000
https://www.thelostsquare.com/
Inviting rooftop bar offers beautiful panoramic views. Handcrafted cocktails and small bites. Outdoor seating.

PEACOCK LOUNGE
37 Whitaker St, Savannah, 912-239-6697
https://flocktothewok.com/peacock-lounge
Exclusive classic cocktail lounge located in the basement level of Flock to the Wok with an alley entrance. Curated cocktails and small bites. Bartenders are real pros.

PLANTERS TAVERN

23 Abercorn St, Savannah, 912-232-4286

www.plantersinnsavannah.com

A dimly lit, low-ceilinged bar in the basement of the high-dollar Olde Pink House, a dignified restaurant in a 1771 house. There's dining room upstairs but downstairs is where all the action is. If you get a seat by the fireplace you might want decide to stay all night and enjoy the live music.

ROCKS ON THE ROOF
102 West Bay St, Savannah, 912-721-3901
https://www.kesslercollection.com/bohemian-savannah/dining/
Located on the rooftop of the Bohemian Hotel Savannah Riverfront, this nice outdoor eatery offers special cocktails, small plates, and incredible views. Live music. Closes at midnight.

SAVANNAH SMILES DUELING PIANOS
314 Williamson St, Savannah, 912-527-6453
https://www.savannahsmilesduelingpianos.com/
High energy piano bar where the show is all-requests playing everything from rock n roll, country, rap, to current tunes. Stop in for dinner and a show or just cocktails. A cash tip will get your request played. Open until 2 a.m.

WET WILLIE'S
101 E River St, Savannah, 912-233-5650
https://www.wetwillies.com/Locations/Savannah-GA-River-Street
Dinner and cocktails or just cocktails to go. Wet Willie's has locations around the globe and are

known for serving the World's Greatest Daiquiris frozen drinks (but not for me—they give me head freeze that ruins my day). Bar menu includes lowest common denominator food items like chicken tenders (more chewy than tender) and gumbo that competes with the gravy at KFC for best wallpaper paste. Cocktails available to go for strolling the waterfront, which helps add to the tackiness of that area.

INDEX

O

P

R

S

T

V

W

Z

www.ingramcontent.com/pod-product-compliance
Ingram Content Group UK Ltd.
Pitfield, Milton Keynes, MK11 3LW, UK
UKHW021644190726
13853UKWH00001B/54